When God's Grace Moves

going through the seasons of life with god's grace

TaShundra Robinson

NOVEMBER MEDIA
PUBLISHING

November Media Publishing, Chicago IL.

Copyright © 2018 TaShundra Robinson

All rights reserved. No part of this publication may be reproduced, distributed, or transmitted in any form or by any means, including photocopying, recording, or other electronic or mechanical methods, without the prior written permission of the publisher, except in the case of brief quotations embodied in critical reviews and certain other noncommercial uses permitted by copyright law. For permission requests, write to the publisher, addressed "Attention: Permissions Coordinator," at the email address below.

November Media Publishing info@novembermediapublishing.com

Ordering Information: Special discounts are available on quantity purchases by corporations, associations, and others. For details, contact the publisher at the email address above.

Printed in the United States of America

Produced & Published by November Media Publishing

ISBN: 978-1-7326897-1-8 (Print Copy)

Scripture references: KJV Bible, English Standard Version, New International Version, and Gods Word Versions

First Edition : November 2018

10 9 8 7 6 5 4 3 2 1

Dedication

I dedicate "When God's Grace Moves" to my parents Robert and Sharon Jones. They introduced me to God at a young age, but allowed me the freedom to pursue Him for myself. Their love for each other poured into the love they had for me and my sisters. My parents displayed the love of Christ in the ways they forgave, supported and encouraged us. God's love was made real through the love of my parents.

Thank you, mom and dad, for being my first examples of how to love like Christ!

Table of Contents

Dedication iii

Trust Your Season 1
   Trust the Process 2
   Pray in God's Grace 6

Grace through Grief 7
   Anointed Comforters 10
   Daily Strength 12
   Pray in God's Grace 15

Grace through Fear 17
   Freedom in Faith 19
   God Is Intentional in All His Ways 22
   Pray in God's Grace 26

Grace through Loneliness 27
   Seek Godly Counsel 29
   Beware of Pride 31
   Comfort in the Comforter 33

Pray in God's Grace *36*

Grace through Growth 37
Obedience Kick-starts Our Blessings *39*
Make Good Use of Everything God Has Given You: *40*
Pray in God's Grace *46*

Grace through Love 47
Spread Love *49*
Know Your Motivation *50*
Pray in God's Grace *54*

Conclusion—Hope 55
He Is Strong Where We Are Weak *56*
Our Response Is Our Responsibility *57*
The Best Decision *60*
Pray in God's Grace *63*

Trust Your Season

"To everything there is a season and a time to every purpose under the Heaven."
Ecclesiastes. 3:1

Imagine preparing for the day by awakening early, selecting your attire for the day, and stepping outside fully bundled with full winter gear, only to realize… it's summer. Life comes in seasons. Each season has a divine timeline designed for our faith and relationship with God to be strengthened. I'd be lost, but for God's grace: grace saves me, grace loves me, grace strengthens me. God has a plan for our lives. In each cycle of life, there is a mission for us to accomplish. In seasons of grief, fear, loneliness, growth, and love, grace is a key element that eases the transition to God's peace. God's grace covers all.

Moses grew up in a foster home. Adopted by Pharaoh's daughter, Moses spent forty years learning the language and customs of the Egyptians. Moses was sent into the desert for another forty years to tend sheep. He didn't question God's guidance when, as the grandson of Pharaoh, God gave him the duties of a shepherd. Yes, he was overqualified, but it was God's will. It was during this season of Moses's life that he learned humility and how to identify with suffering people. He was eighty years old when God brought him to his calling "through the burning bush, Moses! Moses!" (Exodus 3:4). God's message informed Moses he was Israel's deliverer. No moment or experience is ever wasted when we use it wisely. Moses's forty years in a palace prepared him to deal with Pharaoh, and forty years as a shepherd prepared him to lead God's people to their destiny. Without God's grace and power, we are inadequate. God has a way to use wherever we are in life to develop us into the person He intends us to be. God uses our experiences to our good and His glory. The seasons change, but our Lord remains the same.

Trust the Process

Often, we zero in on things that, after closer examination, really aren't that big of a deal. Little problems and concerns are blown out of proportion. Generally, I prefer to know the why, how, and what before I can fully commit to solving a problem. It helps to have an idea of how information will be used, why the situation is important and how long the issue will go on. This isn't how God works. We are placed in situations to grow our faith. Trusting that God has our best interest at heart and knowing that He already has a plan for our lives, we should serve in each season with the goal to glorify the kingdom of God. God knew us before we were conceived and planned for us. (Jeremiah 1:5) Even if our task in a season is not clearly defined, we can strive to love, obey and serve God. Guidance will become clear as we silence the noise and seek God consistently. Each day is an opportunity to give God glory.

Moses chose to trust the process, becoming one of Israel's greatest leaders, a prophet, and a lawgiver. But when he was born, his people were slaves in Egypt, and the Egyptian officials had ordered that all Hebrew baby boys were to be killed. Moses was spared, and Pharaoh's daughter raised Moses. (Exodus 2: 10) God orchestrated each season of Moses's life, ultimately revealing his destiny.

- God directed Moses's path through the people He placed in his life.

Moses ran away to the land of Midian, to escape punishment for killing an Egyptian. In the land of Midian, Moses was rewarded for aiding the daughters of the priest of Midian. Moses dwelled with the priest and became a husband, a father and a shepherd. Moses was trained and humbled by his circumstances. (Exodus 2:15-21)

- God spoke to Moses through a burning bush.

Moses knew he couldn't lead the children of Israel with his own strength. He grew closer to God as he depended on God's grace to provide the right resources to do His will. He was equipped with the rod of God and joined with Aaron. (Exodus 3:2)

- God encouraged Moses during opposition

Moses and Aaron were sent to tell Pharoah to Let God's people go. Pharaoh did not acknowledge or respect the God of Israel. The unhappy result of Moses and Aaron delivering the message to Pharaoh was harder work for the Hebrews.(Exodus 5:1-9)

- God was training Moses to be a leader.

God used Moses, who was a murderer, to deliver the children of Israel out of Egypt. God was willing to show him he could do it. Our past mistakes do not disqualify us from being used by God. (Hebrews 11:24-28)

Moses worried greatly about how the people might respond to him. He could have quit, but he didn't. God could have given up on him, but He didn't. Moses's leadership and spiritual life grew in his obedience to Christ. He was faithful to God's calling to not only deliver Israel but also to prepare the way for the Messiah. The timing of events in our lives is ordained by God to fulfill His purpose. Use the scriptures below to encourage you through the process.

> Now faith is the substance of things hoped for, the evidence of things not seen.
> (Hebrews 11:1)

> For it is God who works in you to will and to act in order to fulfill His good purpose. (Philippians 2:13)

> I will never leave thee, nor forsake thee. (Hebrews 13:5)

> Though I walk in the midst of trouble, You will revive me; You will stretch forth Your hand against the wrath of my enemies, and Your right hand will save me.
> (Psalm 138:7)

I will exalt You, Lord, for You rescued me. You refused to let my enemies triumph over me.
(Psalm 30:1 NLT)

"For I know the plans I have for you," declares the Lord, "plans to prosper you and not to harm you, plans to give you hope and a future."
(Jeremiah 29:11)

May God's grace be with you all.
(Hebrews 13:25)

Pray in God's Grace

Heavenly Father, bless our time together. God, help us see You in every season of our lives. We pray that chains will be broken along this journey. We will recognize that You are with us in the good and difficult times. You never leave nor forsake us. God, we surrender our agendas to do Your will and align our hearts' desires with Your plans for our lives.

Grace through Grief

"The Lord is close to the brokenhearted and saves those who are crushed in spirit."
Psalm 34:18

Though normally (but not always) following God leads to a happier life, and rebelling against God normally (but not always) leads to an unhappy life, God is in control in all situations. In our world invaded by sin, calamity and suffering may come to good and bad alike. Bad things happen because we live in a fallen world. We can be sure, He is all powerful and will be honored we can trust this promise. (Psalm 46:10) By being still we are honoring God and His power and majesty. The joy of the Lord sustains you when situations are going well and when your doubts are high.

We may only associate loss of life with grief; however, grief encompasses any loss. This includes a loss of any meaningful relationship, job, or good health. The first Friday of December 2008, my career as an engineer took a very interesting turn. There had been discussions about a possible reduction, but I'd just been transferred to Greenville, South Carolina. A false sense of security convinced me that the company wouldn't send me home. Wrong. My career with Milliken & Company ended with just under two years in our journey together. They were kind enough to provide a packing company to move me from South Carolina to Birmingham. Even though I'd just purchased a home in LaGrange, Georgia the previous May, there was no reason for me to return to Georgia. I secured a renter for my home in Georgia and moved in with my boyfriend (now husband) and began working as an apartment locator, before enrolling in graduate school in the fall of 2009. Birmingham, Alabama became my home in a stressful manner; however, the journey was blessed by God's grace each step of the way. My last year of graduate school started with a beautiful celebration. I arrived at the Birmingham airport to be greeted by my boyfriend holding a sign with my name on it, welcoming me back to the States from a study abroad program in Cairo, Egypt. As I came closer, he flipped the sign to read the words, "Will you marry me?" My heart was overwhelmed with joy and gratitude. I was finally able to declare that I would gladly marry him! We celebrated our engagement four months later in the very place that we locked eyes for the first time. Much of our family and close friends joined us for the celebration.

The very next day, on October 17th, 2010, we received a call at 11:00 p.m. that turned our world upside down. My mother had a massive heart attack and was no longer alive. My biggest cheerleader, my confidant, my mommy was no longer going to be able to encourage me from this place. Only God knows exactly why things happen as they do. We made the plans for my mom's home going and pursued the process of living in our new normal.

The season was hard, but six weeks later the season became harder. While en route to celebrate my sister-in-law's birthday, we were notified that my father was in a fatal car accident. My father and I had just spoken that morning and he'd encouraged me that our new normal would take some time, but we would get through it together. In this moment, my joy was temporarily deflated from my body.

God's grace is our life support when we are unable to see past the present moments. Ruth is a great example of how trusting the presence of God can carry you through any season. Ruth found God by observing the actions of her mother-in-law, Naomi. In spite of being widowed and losing both her sons, Naomi trusted God. Yes, she had moments of sadness and despair, but she kept her faith. Ruth took note of how Naomi lived and when Ruth's husband passed away, she clung closer to her mother-in-law. Ruth made her intentions clear saying, "Entreat me not to leave thee, or to return from following after thee: "I will go; and where thou lodgest, I will lodge: thy people shall be my people, and thy God my God (Ruth 1:16). Ruth's decision to leave her hometown, her comforts and familiar people made space for God to bless her life beyond her wildest dreams.

Anointed Comforters

In the midst of Naomi's grief, God sent her daughter-in-law to bless her. Naomi gave Ruth the opportunity to stay in her hometown of Moab, but Ruth saw the hope in Naomi's life and desired it for her own. Naomi lost her husband and both her sons, yet God was doing a mighty work in her life through Ruth. Ruth saw God in Naomi's everyday actions. The family had ten years to grow and learn each other's ways, and over this time Ruth observed enough of Naomi's character to decide, in her grief, that she wanted to follow Naomi. Naomi loved and cared for Ruth. Her strength and love, after losing her husband and sons, served as a powerful witness to God's grace. In the midst of sorrow, we must remain available to receive God's blessings. We do not know God's plan for our lives, but we can rest assured that God has a plan. God has a unique way of placing His children along the right path to bless one another. Society would have it that mothers-in-law would not have the ability to relate to their daughters-in-laws. A typical relationship between "the in-laws" is assumed to be difficult and strained, but we don't have to accept that in our own lives. Ruth did not allow the lie of society to block her from following Naomi, leaving her home and seeking a relationship with God for herself.

God was at work in Ruth's life. The pursuit of grace led Ruth to the fields of Boaz to glean ears of corn. It was the harvest season of wheat and barley, and reapers were hired to cut down the stalks and tie them into bundles. Israelite law established that any grain that was dropped was left for the gleaners, poor people who picked it up and used it for food. Ruth was willing to work hard, and God had gone before her to provide a place and provision, putting her in the position to receive her blessing for meeting him halfway. Instead of depending on Naomi to provide for her, Ruth took the initiative to provide for their new family. Ruth displayed humility, perseverance, and hope. Ruth was blessed because of her faithfulness to God. Her daily obedience placed her in position to bless her mother-in-law, herself and her future descendants. God has a way of putting us in positions that allow us to decide how to respond. Will we seek counsel from Him? Will we trust Him? Will we lean on His promises? We may not understand why situations are as they are, but we can find peace in knowing that the All-Knowing is at work.

Daily Strength

The deaths of my parents exposed me to a deep loss that I'd never imagined I would feel at twenty-five years old. But I leaned heavily on the foundation in Christ they'd shared with me in my youth. My foundation in God graced me with the strength to breathe through each day and fully participate in life. "So do not throw away your confidence; it will be richly rewarded. You need to persevere so that when you have done the will of God, you will receive what

He has promised." (Hebrews 10: 35-36 NIV) We were still planning our wedding, which was two months away at this point, and my graduate semester was coming to an end. My days were hard, but I could not quit. God strategically placed many special family members and friends in my life. On the days that I couldn't find the right words to describe my day, I didn't have to. My tears were met with acceptance and understanding. God comforted me through His grace and mercy. John 14:1 says, "Let not your heart be troubled: ye believe in God, believe also in me." No tragedy is beyond God's sovereignty.

To persevere through my pains, I worked toward acceptance of this harsh reality. It was difficult, yet necessary to meditate on the joyful events occurring in my life. While I had many things going on to keep my mind "busy," it was more freeing to be in the presence of God building His kingdom. My husband and I are very involved in our local church and during this challenging time, we were consistently being fed the word of God. In addition to being nourished spiritually, we activated the word by being the feet and hands of Jesus. We hosted small groups, served on volunteer teams, and shared the gospel with our friends and family. The desire, strength, and willingness to accept our new normal was only made possible through God continually showering His grace. The same grace that was available to me during that time is available for you. Find comfort in the scriptures below when going through a difficult season.

> He will wipe every tear from their eyes. There will be no more death or mourning or crying or pain, for the old order of things has passed away.
> (Revelation 21:4 NIV)

> Why are you downcast, O my soul? Why so disturbed within me? Put your hope in God, for I will yet praise Him. My Savior and my God.
> (Psalm 43:5 NIV)

> But He said to me, "My grace is sufficient for you, for my power is made perfect in your weakness." Therefore, I will boast all the more gladly about my weaknesses, so that Christ's power may rest on me.
> (2 Corinthians 12:9 NIV)

> The Lord gives strength to His people; the Lord blesses His people with peace.
> (Psalm 29:11 NIV)

Therefore, I take pleasure in infirmities, in reproaches, in necessities, in persecutions, in distress for Christ's sake: for when I am weak, then am I strong.

(2 Co 12:10)

Pray in God's Grace

Heavenly Father, we know that in You there will be no more death. Thank You for being the hope for the hopeless, and a father for the fatherless. God, as we come to You with our troubles, You lovingly shower us with Your Grace and mercy. God, it is my prayer that anyone who is struggling with a loss of any nature will cling to You. Reveal the areas in our lives that can be used to minister to others. I pray that any voids in our lives will be filled with Your love. I pray we commit ourselves to Your will. You are the source of our joy. Dear Lord, I pray that You shower us with Your peace and purpose in Your Spirit, as we partner with You to live in Your will.

Grace through Fear

"Fear thou not; for I am with thee: be not dismayed; for I am thy God: I will strengthen thee; yea, I will help thee; yea, I will uphold thee with the right hand of my righteousness."
– Isaiah 41:10

When Naomi arrived back to Bethlehem, she was confronted by many from her past. Naomi and her family had been gone for over ten years. Many trials had come her way and she was bitter; her hardships weighed heavily on her. Naomi didn't identify as herself, she asked to be addressed as Mara (Ruth 1:20). She left Israel married and secure, only to return poor and widowed. The fear in her life was very evident. In our times of fear, we can get bogged down in the pain and lose sight of the people and resources that are in our lives to bless us. Ruth was there as a part of God's amazing plan to bless

Naomi... Naomi was a widow and was just returning to her homeland from the Moab, she was afraid. The grace of God blessed Ruth to be compassionate and loving in Naomi's season of fear. Never once did Ruth try to talk Naomi out of what she was feeling. Ruth loved her through her difficult period, and they were both blessed for it.

"Rob, something isn't right." This Sunday morning I woke up before my alarm, knowing that something was a bit off. I found myself startled by the unwelcome sight of blood. At the time, I was eleven weeks pregnant, so immediately I was overwhelmed with fear. The situation was oh so familiar, as we had just experienced a similar scenario in September 2016. While the thought of having another miscarriage brought so many emotions, I rejected the feeling of hopelessness. My hope was not crushed by what my eyes could see. The reality of the situation was that we were having our second miscarriage in a year. The Holy Spirit comforted me with "Peace I leave with you, my peace I give unto you: not as the world giveth give I unto you. Let not your heart be troubled, neither let it be afraid" (John 14:27). Despite the current situation, at that time, God's peace was so strong within me.

Freedom in Faith

As the disciples followed Jesus into the boat, waves swept over the boat with fury. The disciples found Jesus sleeping and awoke Him saying, "Lord, save us! We're going to drown!" In the throes of this furious storm, Jesus was sleeping. Jesus replied, "You of little faith, why are you so afraid?" Jesus rose and rebuked the winds and the waves, and it was completely calm (Matt 8: 23-27). Fear gripped the disciples and blinded the men from having faith in the ultimate protector.

God designed us to trust in Him and know that we are made for His purpose and can conquer all things through Christ. Fear has many ways to manifest itself in our lives. Four of these manifestations are:

1. Anxiety

2. Anger

3. Confusion

4. Isolation

Each of these states are results of fear and are in direct conflict with the freedom granted to us through Jesus

Christ. It may not be initially obvious, but these emotions are stirred up by fear. When we invite God into our emotional struggles, His grace will turn it around.

Anxiety: "Don't worry about anything, instead, pray about everything. Tell God what you need, and thank Him for all He has done. Then you will experience God's peace, which exceeds anything we can understand. His peace will guard your hearts and minds as you live in Christ Jesus." (Phil 4: 6-7) "Don't worry" sounds unreasonable considering the many variables that impact our daily lives; however, by God's grace, we can surrender. Paul reminds us that our worries should be turned into prayers.

Anger: "He that is slow to anger is better than the mighty, and he that ruleth his spirit than he that taketh a city." (Prov. 16:32) It is a great personal victory to control our tempers. Self-control is superior to conquest. A heated exchange stands the risk of jeopardizing so much. Relationships and jobs can be negatively impacted. Losing control can easily cause us to forfeit many of the people or things we don't want to live without.

Confusion: We cannot be wise and confused at the same time. Foolishness leads to disorder, but wisdom leads to peace and goodness. True wisdom can be measured by one's character. Being envious of a classmates new car, a co-worker's promotion or a relatives new home prevents us from appreciating the blessings in our own lives. James warns that where envying and strife is, there is confusion and every evil work. (James 3:16) Confusion prevents true progress in improved relationships and personal growth in our lives. To avoid the contamination of confusion, identify it fast and eliminate it.

"For God is not the author of confusion, but of peace, as in all churches of the saints." (1 Corinthians 14:33)

Isolation: Ecclesiastes 4:9-10 says, "Two are better than one because they have a good return for their work: if one falls down, his friend can help him up. But pity the man who falls and has no one to help him up!" Isolation causes us to think that we are right to not answer the door or to ignore the person calling to check in on our well-being. In our minds, isolation is the solution to avoid facing the world when we have regrets. While in isolation, negative thoughts take over your mind and could lead to loss of reality, depression, or strained relationships e. We are not designed to be alone. We are called to rejoice with those who rejoice and weep with those who weep. (Romans 12:15)

Companionship and intimacy take work, but it's worth it. We are on this earth to serve God and one another.

Fear operates as a distraction from the true purpose God has for us and disturbs any progress that was being gained. When battling fear, it's important we catch ourselves quickly and speak life over the lies the enemy is yelling. The quicker you turn back to the important task you're completing, the less time will be wasted.

The truth is we don't have to fear any situation. We tend to feel the most fear when we have halfway surrendered to a situation. When we still have our hands in finding a solution or "working it out" is when we fear the most. There are countless messages from God in the Bible encouraging us not to fear. This does not mean we shouldn't be afraid, but that we should trust God with our fears when they come. We can take heart, for God has overcome the world (John 16:33).

God Is Intentional in All His Ways

When we are at our lowest, God is still working in our favor. We must draw closer to God in these times. The closer we get to God, the more wisdom and discernment we're graced with. As we gain more discernment and wisdom, we act more thoughtfully. Along this journey, our response to difficult times should be to have faith in God's promises.

To increase our faith:

(1) Get closer to God. "Come near to God and He will come near to you." (James 4:8)

Spend quality and consistent time with God's word. Time with God builds a better relationship. When we feel close we feel secure. Security only comes when we know what God's word promises for our lives.

(2) Nurture your relationship. "Humble yourselves before the Lord and He will lift you up." (James 4:10)

Spending time in prayer is where we give devotion to God. We get direction from God, during our prayer time. We grow in our faith, increase our trust and declare our dependence in Him by spending time with God. The presence of the Lord increases in our lives, as we recognize that our validation comes from God alone. Despite our shortcomings, God fills us with worth and dignity.

(3) Learn to hear God's voice: "Behold, I stand at the door and knock. If anyone hears my voice and opens the door,

I will come in to him and eat with him, and he with me." (Revelation 3:20) In our quality time, God's voice becomes clearer. Jesus is knocking on the door of our hearts. We should turn to God daily and trust His word.

"God works out all things for the good to them that love God." (Rom 8:28) This does not mean that everything that happens to us will feel good immediately. But God is able to defeat the evil that is present and work all things out for our future. Happiness is a byproduct of God's work in our lives, but not the primary focus. Only when we acknowledge our love for God, can we know that He is working to keep us in position to fulfill His purpose.

A mindset of trusting God leads to a renewed perspective on life. Life's treasures or earthly securities will not provide peace. When we set our sights on Heaven, the troubles of the world do not overcome us. God has reassured us in John 16:33 that we can take heart, knowing that God has overcome the world. As Jesus spoke to the disciples, He confirmed that trouble will come. During our struggles, our comforter is with us. Remember the victory has been granted to every child of God, we can claim the peace of Christ in the most troublesome times.

The only weapon the enemy has are lies. Replace the lies of the enemy with the truth in God's word.

For God did not give us a spirit of timidity, but a spirit of power, of love and of self-discipline.
(2 Timothy 1:7 NIV)

The righteous cry out, and the Lord hears them; He delivers them from all their troubles. The Lord is close to the brokenhearted and saves those who are crushed in spirit.
(Psalm 34:17-18 NIV)

When I am afraid, I will put my trust in You. In God, whose word I praise, In God I have put my trust; I shall not be afraid. What can mere man do to me?
(Psalm 56:3-4)

Have no fear of sudden disaster or of the ruin that overtakes the wicked, for the Lord will be your confidence and will keep your foot from being snared.
(Proverbs 3:25-26 NIV)

It is for freedom that Christ has set us free. Stand firm, then, and do not let yourselves be burdened again by a yoke of slavery. (Galatians 5:1)

He who dwells in the shelter of the Most High will rest in the shadow of the Almighty. I will say of the Lord, "He is my refuge, my fortress, my God, in whom I trust."
(Psalm 91:1-2)

He will cover you with His feathers and under His wings you will find refuge; His faithfulness will be your shield and rampart.
(Psalm 9:4)

Pray in God's Grace

Lord, we thank You that You are our confidence. We find refuge in Your presence. Our strength and freedom come from You. Help us serve You better by knowing that You are close to the brokenhearted and remain strong in Your loving arms. We declare victory over the enemy of fear, anxiety, isolation, confusion, and anger. God, you are bigger and greater. We trust You and know that we are victorious in Christ Jesus.

Grace through Loneliness

"The Lord is my rock, and my fortress, and my deliverer, my God, my strength, in whom I will trust; my buckler, and the horn of my salvation, and my high tower."
Psalm 18:2

When our circumstances don't make sense to us, we can isolate ourselves by being envious of others and creating insecurities. Insecurities create the illusion of lack of self-worth and are a trick of the devil. God does not maintain a list of our many sins (Psalm 130:3-4). He sets the example for us as His children, to quickly and fully forgive others. When God completely forgives us, He removes the wall that unforgiveness creates. We can approach God with no shame. If not for God's grace, where would I be?

A few illusions insecurity creates in relationships:

- The illusion that we are always being talked about.

- The illusion that everyone around us knows more than we do.

- The illusion that it's too hard to forgive.

These are all lies from the enemy. These selfish ambitions disguised as insecurities convince us that we are not able nor worthy of God's blessings. In truth, God's grace provides all the qualification we need. His sacrifice on the cross granted us access to live in freedom through Christ. When we are wronged, we are inclined to seek vengeance; however, God teaches us that the saying an "eye for an eye" is not the way to resolve issues. He tells us in Matthew 5:38-39 we should resist evil and turn the other cheek. This is a clear expression of God's mercy. Choosing to give love and forgiveness over offense takes supernatural strength that can only come from God. The Holy Spirit guides us in the way of righteousness. (John 16:13) Get freedom from insecurities by praying for those who have caused pain in our lives and depend on God to reconcile our hearts.

Seek Godly Counsel

In the times of uncertainty, everyone will not understand. Everyone is not meant to give counsel. God says, "Eyes have not seen, nor have ears heard, nor mind conceived what God has prepared for those who love Him." (1 Corinthians 2:9) No one on this earth, including ourselves, can fathom what's in store for our lives. It is important to seek godly counsel in times of confusion. Sometimes it's easier to go to close friends or relatives, but know that traits like being judgmental or pessimistic can lead our thoughts to places God never intended them to go. The wrong response to our experiences can cause more confusion and not aid in the clarity we need to get to the finish line. Ruth was foreign, but she knew where her support came from. When she experienced Boaz's grace, Ruth sought counsel from Naomi. Ruth knew Naomi's commitment was to do the will of God and that she could trust her guidance. Naomi guided Ruth to uncover Boaz's feet and lie near them to express her interest in him being her kinsman-redeemer. Naomi's advice was not a seductive act, but an Israelite custom and law. It was common for servants to lie at the feet of their master. Ruth was showing Boaz that he was welcome to find someone to marry her or marry her himself. Ruth played her role well as a helper to Naomi. She unselfishly worked hard and learned the customs of the land. As she was adapting to the new land, it was God's grace that surrounded her with protection, guidance, and encouragement from Naomi. In our journeys, it's imperative to know who God has placed in our lives to support us.

"Where there is no counsel, the people fall; but in the multitude of counselors there is safety." (Proverbs 11:14) We are not on this journey alone. Regardless if our loneliness is caused by fear, anger or regret, we should not give up on seeking godly relationships. Instead of isolating ourselves, we should trust God. God is always with us and waiting for us to draw near to Him. He is our helper and the sustainer of our souls. (Psalm 54:4) We may feel misunderstood, but we have to take captive any negative thoughts and make them obedient to Christ. (2 Corinthians 10: 4-5) God has strategically placed people in our lives to be blessed or to bless us. We all have a purpose and have work to do. Seek godly counsel and finish strong.

If Ruth would have allowed her circumstances in a strange land to keep her from going into the fields to work, she would have missed to the opportunity of meeting Boaz, changing her life, and becoming the ancestor of a king and the Messiah. She had every reason to feel insecure and disqualify herself from the job. She knew that foreigners were not typically warmly welcomed by all in the land, but she was indeed warmly welcomed by the one person God sent to change her life. Ruth's reputation for showing kindness and generosity to others preceded her. Boaz took note of her character and was impressed by her hard work.

Beware of Pride

Pride steals contentment, cheats us of vision and demands we go our own way. A life packed with materialistic pursuits deafens us to God's word. Pride was also present in the early church. Ananias and his wife, Sapphira saw the blessings showered on others for selling property and donating the money to believers in need. Ananias and Sapphira were blinded by pride when they decided to sell their possession and keep back part of the price. They arranged to take advantage of the church. Pride snuck in disguised as greed, leading the couple to cheat the church from the proceeds from selling their land. Peter exposed their sin, saying, "Thou hast not lied unto men, but unto God." Ananias and Sapphira dropped dead as a result of their sin (Acts 5:1 -5). The sin committed was not stinginess, but lying to God and God's people, saying they gave the whole amount but holding back some for themselves and pretending to be more generous than they really were. This act was judged harshly because dishonesty and covetousness are destructive in a church. Pride has a sneaky way of disguising itself as something good for us and can lead to making us pay an unnecessary and sometimes extreme consequence. We can be blinded from all that God has for our lives by letting pride get in the way.

The enemy is counting on us to discount our blessings. Comparison to others is one of the many ways this occurs. When we look around rather than look up, we silence God's promises and give extra volume to the lies of the enemy. The couple's error continued when they convinced themselves they could provide for themselves better than God could. We don't have to cheat ourselves out of our blessings. Our focus on Heaven will keep our perspective in line with God's purpose for our journey. We delay our blessings when we are: (1) focusing on our own agendas, (2) looking down on others, or (3) thinking God's blessings are from our own merits.

The apostle Paul shared a word in Ephesians 6:11, 14-17 that lays out how we can protect ourselves against the tricks of the enemy: "Put on the whole armor of God," to "stand against the wiles of the devil." Stand protected with: the belt of truth, the breastplate of righteousness, the shoes of gospel peace, the shield of faith, the helmet of salvation, and the sword of the spirit, which is the word of God. Our help and protection come solely from God.

Comfort in the Comforter

Peace. The peace the world gives has nothing on the peace granted by God. As the Holy Spirit works in our lives, deep lasting peace overcomes our everyday living. Peace is deeper than the absence of conflict, thinking positively or feeling good. Since my parent's deaths, God has revealed His hand in my life in many ways. Four months after my father's death, I married a wonderful man Robert Joe Robinson, III. Robert was my father's name. Ten months after our wedding, we were blessed with a beautiful princess Zora Antoinette Robinson. Zora was my grandmother's name and is my mother-in-law's name. Just before Zora turned two, God blessed us with a prince Robert Joe Robinson, IV. I am amazed at how much our kids display so many of my parent's qualities. Zora is deeply caring, outspoken and loves to worship God. Her loving ways remind me so much of my mother. Robert (IV) has brought me to tears with how similar he is to my father when he praises God to worship music, his honesty and the unique way he crosses his legs. God has continuously been working in our lives, blessing our careers, leading us to a great church, providing supportive family and friends, and revealing our purpose in marriage ministries. In spite of our recent losses, we cling to our hope in Heaven. God graces us with the strength to enjoy the journey, peacefully.

As Christians, we have access to the weapons of God: prayer, faith, hope, love, the Holy Spirit and God's word. These weapons help us fight for and maintain our peace in Christ. We're at peace when we experience the true confidence that any circumstance in our lives will work out for our good, knowing that our destiny is set because we have the victory over sin. Meditate on the scriptures below and be reminded of God's gifted peace.

> Let all bitterness and wrath and anger and clamor and slander be put away from you, along with malice. Be kind to one another, tender-hearted, forgiving each other, just as God in Christ also has forgiven you.
> (Ephesians 4: 31-32)

Strive for peace with everyone, and for the holiness without which no one will see the Lord. See to it that no one fails to obtain the grace of God; that no "root of bitterness" springs up and causes trouble, and by it many become defiled.
(Hebrews 12: 14-15 ESV)

Trust in the Lord with all thine heart; and lean not unto thine own understanding.
(Proverbs 3:5)

And the peace of God, which passeth all understanding, shall keep your hearts and minds through Christ Jesus.
(Philippians 4:7)

Peace I leave with you, my peace I give unto you: not as the world giveth, give I unto you. Let not your heart be troubled, neither let it be afraid.
(John 14:27)

As those who have been chosen of God, holy and beloved, put on a heart of compassion, kindness, humility, gentleness, and patience; bearing with one another, and forgiving each other, whoever has a complaint against anyone; just as the Lord forgave you, so also should you.
(Colossians 3:12-13)

Casting down imaginations, and every high thing that exalteth itself against the knowledge of God, and bringing into captivity every thought to the obedience of Christ. (2 Corinthians 10:5)

Pray in God's Grace

Heavenly Father, we lean on Your word to guide us in the way we should go. We ask that any distractions in our lives are silenced to allow us to hear better from You. Right now, we align our agendas with Your peaceful agenda for our lives. Just as You forgive us daily and fully, we seek the strength and grace to forgive those who have hurt us. Father, help us find peace in Your promises.

Grace through Growth

"Put on your new nature, and be renewed as you learn to know your Creator and become like Him."
(Colossians 3:10)

As Christians, we are ever evolving. The more we know and live out God's ways, the more He changes us. Because the process is lifelong, we should never cease learning and obeying His word. There are incentives to actively seeking to grow in God's word. The grapevine is symbolic in the Old Testament. It symbolizes the fruitfulness in doing God's work on earth. We are reminded of the fruitfulness of our spiritual heritage in Isaiah 51: 1-7: Abraham was only one person, but much came from his faithfulness. By choosing to be faithful, we ensure that God's blessings will be felt for generations to come. There is such great value in being obedient to God's word. God is faithful to His promises and the word shows us, as we draw near to Him, He blesses us. Obedience bears the fruit of growth. Growth requires passion, proactiveness, and persistence.

(1) Passion is fueled by more than a thought. It is a burning desire to complete a task all while enjoying the journey. There is no bitterness in passion. When our motivation is to live God's purpose for our lives, passion is the response that will fuel us along.

"Yes, Lord, walking in the way of your laws, we wait for you; your name and renown are the desire of our hearts." (Isaiah 26:8)

(2) Living proactively keeps us prepared rather than mindless reactions. Living each day with intention is a proactive way to honor God's call on our lives and have a sustaining impact for the kingdom. "The plans of the diligent lead to profit as surely as haste leads to poverty." (Proverbs 21:5)

(3) Persistence means we do not run when times get tough. Things will not be jolly every day, but we have to know that the joy of the Lord is our strength. True joy transcends the ups and downs of life. A growing relationship with the Lord increases our joy, and it helps us walk through

adversity without giving in when the going gets tough. The joy of living with Jesus Christ daily helps you maintain your joy no matter how good or bad the situation. God says, "These things have I spoken unto you, that my joy might remain in you, and that your joy might be full." (John 15: 11)

With passion for Christ, being intentional and persistent we can know Christ, be like Christ and be all Christ has called us to be.

Obedience Kick-starts Our Blessings

God has all types of blessings in store for us, but it's up to us to claim them. We aren't able to unlock them all when we aren't being obedient. Keep Christ first and do what's right. Words of wisdom - Granddaddy. The book of Ruth is the perfect example of the impact our obedience can have on our blessings and the blessing of generations. Ruth took the first step to seek God, after observing her mother-in-law's life of love with God. Ruth was a Moabitess, but she found hope in the one true God and followed His ways for her life. She was blessed because of her faithfulness. Ruth and Naomi came to Bethlehem as poor widows, but they soon became prosperous through Ruth's marriage to Boaz.

(Ruth 4:10) Ruth's obedience carried blessings to generations to come, as she became the great-grandmother of King David. God's grace and protection were all over the lives of Naomi and Ruth.

Make Good Use of Everything God Has Given You:

It may seem that we are justified in our desires to not want to get out of bed or to not have the energy to read a little longer, but we must be aware that we are operating in our own strength in those times. God's grace provides and gives us the breath of life that we need. He is our source. We must guard ourselves against laziness. Proverbs says in 12:24, "The hand of the diligent shall bear rule: but the slothful shall be under tribute." We must be diligent in our ways and make good use of our resources and possessions. Waste is a sign of laziness and is poor stewardship. I believe what God says about my life. I cannot trust my feelings. My feelings tell me that "I am how I am and It's okay." But God's word says I am more than a conqueror. (Rom 8:37) I trust God's word over my feelings. I recently completed a personality survey to better understand my work habits. The results were interesting, but overall, I counter the results with the word of God.

- My personality says I'm spontaneous.
  - I must learn to be consistent.
  - I must push through and be intentional even when I want to just go with the flow.
  - I must know that I am more effective when I take my plans to God first and allow Him to bless and align them with His plans for me.
- What should my message be?
- Who needs to be blessed by my message?
- How should I deliver my message?
- I don't like to plan.
  - Being prepared is going to God first.
  - Planning is taking the time to listen to God and having a rough draft of how things should flow.
  - Leave room for the Holy Spirit to have its way.
  - Grow through it.

We do not have to find our identity in what the world says about us. Personality tests have always been a struggle for me because the results have the ability to "justify" ways that may not align with who God says we are. Inviting His grace in our daily lives is the best way to work the kinks out.

Do you believe that God wants to bless us? When we choose to trust God's promises for our lives and know that His grace will carry us through, God blesses our paths. God proclaims, "I am the light of the world. Whoever follows me will never walk in darkness, but will have the light of light" (John 8:12). The decision to put the keys to our lives in God's hands and surrender our agenda sets us on a path to ultimately be blessed. To follow God, we must abandon our own agendas. Our will must align with God's will for our lives to do His work. To remind ourselves who is in control, biblical affirmations can keep our minds fixed on God's promises. A few of my favorite affirmations are:

- Before I formed you in the womb I knew you, before you were born I set you apart. (Jeremiah 1:5)

- Be strong and courageous. Do not be afraid; do not be discouraged, for the Lord your God will be with you wherever you go. (Joshua 1:9)

- I can do all things through Christ who strengthens me. (Phil 4:13)

- I will not leave you as orphans; I will come to you. (John 14:18)

- Peace I leave with you; my peace I give you. I do not give to you as the world gives. Do not let your hearts be troubled and do not be afraid. (John 14: 27)

- God works his power best in my weakness. (2 Corinthians 12:9)

As we recall, the story of Ruth and Naomi begins with two widows living in poverty. Ruth's obedience to God's plan for her life. Her decision to leave Moab created an opportunity to get closer to God, be a blessing to Naomi, and meet her future husband. Boaz wanted to pursue Ruth honorably, by going to the kinsman with first rights to marry Ruth and continue the family legacy. He explained that the land would be the kinsman's to own, but he would also have to marry the widow to maintain the name of the dead with his property (Ruth 4:5). Boaz was aware of his intentions to marry Ruth, and he chose his words strategically.

The thought of acquiring the widow of Elimelech and her daughter-in-law caused the kinsman to rethink his need for the property. Ultimately, he did not want to interrupt his own estate. The kinsman walked away from the property and missed the blessing God had in store for Ruth's husband. To receive God's guidance, we must acknowledge God in all we do. Ruth married the wealthiest and most respected man in the town. God redeemed and transformed Ruth. She became part of the ancestry of Christ gave birth to a son named Obed, the father of Jesse, the father of David. Ruth gave her life to God and reaped the harvest from the seeds she sowed. (Ruth 4:13-16)

Ruth would have never found Boaz if she left Naomi.

One test can lead you to your blessing in the next season. Life is full of tests and blessings, and we don't get to have one without the other. For her faithfulness Ruth was blessed:

1. With a husband and son. (Ruth 4:13)

2. To renew life in her mother-in-law. (Ruth 4:14-15)

3. To become a part of the genealogy of Jesus Christ. (Matt 1: 1-6)

Anyone who meets a testing challenge head-on and manages to stick it out is mighty fortunate. For such persons, loyally in love with God, the reward is life and more life. (James 1:12 MSG)

We can talk ourselves out of our blessings. When we seek first our own agenda, we will miss out on the full blessing God has for us. Selfish ambitions are not of God. Being selfish will hinder our ability to be fully effective for the kingdom. We must ask ourselves: (1) What are my priorities? (2) Where is God on my list? (3) What does His word say? God will clearly guide us when we make Him a vital part of everything that we do. Someone's salvation is depending on our obedience. God's word can set us back on the path of His purpose for our lives.

But those who trust in the Lord for help will find their strength renewed. They will rise on wings like eagles; they will run and not get weary; they will walk and not grow weak. (Isaiah 40:31)

Let your hope keep you joyful, be patient in your troubles, and pray at all times.
(Romans 12:12)

Do not merely listen to the word, do what it says
(James 1:22 NIV)

So Ruth went out to gather grain behind the harvesters. And as it happened, she found herself working in a field that belonged to Boaz, the relative of her father-in-law, Elimelech.
(Ruth 2: 3 NLT)

See which part of the field they are harvesting, and then follow them. I have warned the young men not to treat you roughly. And when you are thirsty, help yourself to the water they have drawn from the well.
(Ruth 2: 9 NLT)

He must become greater, I must become less. (Jn 3:30)

Pray in God's Grace

Heavenly Father, thank You for being our ultimate provider. God, we pray to be overcome by Your joy and peace. Please continue to bless us with provision and favor in our assigned fields and take the initiative to reach out to help the hurting. Renew our purpose for our lives, so that we may follow You fully. Father, please bless our obedience.

Grace through Love

"We love Him because He first loved us."
(1 John 4:19)

The ultimate expression of love came from our Savior. He loved us enough to sacrifice His Son for us. Jesus is our example of what it means to love. "For God made Christ, who never sinned, to be the offering for our sin so that we could be made right with God through Christ." (2 Corinthians 5:21) God gave His life, rather than give up on our lives. Nobody has ever or will ever love us as much as God. God calls us to love one another and love never fails.

When God's love and our love come together, others see Christ in us.

As Ruth was blessed by Boaz's good graces, she questioned what she'd done to deserve his kindness, reminding him she was "only a foreigner" (Ruth 2:10-11). Boaz replied, "Yes, I know, but I also know about everything you have done for your mother-in-law since the death of your husband. I have heard how you left your father and mother and your own land to live here among complete strangers." Boaz's love for Ruth was full of compassion, caring, and concern for her well-being.

Relationships are investments and present many opportunities to get closer to God while learning to love like Jesus. There are times my husband and I misunderstand each other. Usually, this occurs when we are stressed or when there are unspoken expectations between us. While it is expected that we will have disagreements we work hard to limit those occurrences. We keep God first, strive to maintain open and honest communication, and exercise empathy. Having God first keeps our intentions pure. Honest communication is a catalyst for mature connections. Meeting the needs of the other is enhanced by displaying empathy. Maintaining healthy relationships is easier when everyone's needs are met. It is more challenging to share in a relationship when you're tired, upset or overwhelmed. The grace of God fills in where we fall short.

Spread Love

The Holy Spirit gives us the power to love and it's our duty to put it to good use. There are times it may seem we have every right to not show love, but we are wrong. We are to love as God loves and love the person even when they are not living in a godly way. Dislike the sin and love the person. As Jesus sat to teach in the Mount of Olives, he was brought a woman caught in adultery. The leaders used the law of Moses as their basis to stone the adulterous woman. Attempting to trick Jesus into violating the law of Moses, the leaders were sent away sheepishly when prompted by Jesus, "He who is without sin cast the first stone." (Jn 8:7). This is a significant statement about judging others. Because He upheld the legal penalty for adultery, stoning, Jesus could not be accused of acting against the law. But by saying that only those without sin could throw the first stone, He highlighted the importance of compassion and forgiveness. This story also emphasizes the fact that none of us are without sin, and to pass judgment on others is to act as though we have never sinned. God is the one and only judge. Jesus didn't condemn the woman accused of adultery, but neither did He condone her sin. She was told to go and sin no more. Jesus is ready and willing to forgive any sin in our lives, but confession and repentance mean a change of heart. The grace of God is the way to transform our hearts from our sinful natures.

Know Your Motivation

It's hard to give what you don't have. Have you received the love of Christ? Any good relationship works best with reciprocated love. But in order to give love, we first have to receive love. In first John, the apostle John uses the phrase "Beloved" to address the congregation throughout various verses. Simplifying this word as Be – Loved means John was further encouraging the congregation to see themselves as God sees us. We are loved, and all that's left is acceptance of that love. This kind of love isn't just a feeling; it's a way of life. To love like Christ is a choice followed through with action. As 1 Corinthians 13: 4-7 shows, love is patient, kind, does not envy, is not proud or rude, does not keep record of being wronged, and best of all love does NOT give up! Love is always hopeful. Love without expecting anything in return from anyone, this is servant love. Our expectations should be in Christ alone. God's kind of love is unselfish, and it can only be possible to love this way with His help. The closer we come to Christ, the more capacity we have to love others.

1 John 4:8 says "God is Love," not "Love is God." We can confuse the root of love, which contaminates the purpose of love. God's love for us was to enable us to love others. Love is a winning strategy. Love explains (1) why God creates, (2) why God cares, (3) why we are free to choose, (4) why Christ died, as His love for us caused Him to seek a solution to the problem of sin, and (5) why we receive eternal life. When we love God's way we are vulnerable to others, but there's no need to fear being vulnerable. God speaks of servant love as giving a cup of water to a thirsty child, a model of unselfish service. (Matthew 10:42) God notices every good deed we do or don't do as if He were the one receiving it. Loving **God's way isn't easy, but with His grace it's possible.**

Defined and realistic expectations are essential means of communication in any relationship. One afternoon, I picked my son up from school and the first question out of his mouth was, "Do you have a snack for me?" His expectation was clear. Unfortunately, I did not have this well-anticipated snack. Without a second thought, he completely melted down. He was four, just for perspective. In that moment, I had a choice. Actually several choices. But I knew he had this expectation because this wasn't his first time making it very clear. While that did not excuse his response, it did engage my compassion for his disappointment. I chose peace in the situation because I understood his heart's desires had been communicated and set. Our response to the expectations set by others is just as important as the communication of those expectations. In Psalm 37:4, David encourages us that God will give us the desires of our hearts. We have an opportunity to love like Christ and care about what matters to those we love. Our preparation for their expectation is just as impactful as the response to their disappointment. Disappointment can interfere with our ability to love fully and consistently, but if we follow the example set by Christ we see that love is a winning strategy. God's word below illustrates how love works in our lives.

> May the Lord, the God of Israel, under whose wings you have come to take refuge, reward you fully for what you have done.
> (Ruth 2:12 NLT)

> I will give you the right words and such wisdom that none of your opponents will be able to reply or refute you!
> (Luke 21:15 NLT)

But love your enemies, do good to them, and lend to
them without expecting to get anything back.
Then your reward will be great. (Luke 6: 35)

In this was manifested the love of God toward us,
because that God sent His only begotten Son into the
world, that we might live through Him.
(1 John 4:9)

Let us therefore come boldly unto the throne of grace,
that we may obtain mercy, and find grace to
help in time of need.
(Hebrews 4:16)

Let love and faithfulness never leave you; bind them
around your neck, write them on the tablet of your heart.
Then you will win favor and a good name in the sight of
God and man.
(Proverbs 3:3)

When you have eaten and are satisfied, praise the Lord
your God, for the good land He has given you.
(Deuteronomy 8:10)

Pray in God's Grace

Heavenly Father, we are called to love Your children as You love us. We come boldly to Your throne asking for the strength to love others the way You so graciously love us. Please give us the wisdom and strength to love without expecting anything in return. God, let Your grace in tough situations serve as a constant reminder of our goodness.

Conclusion—Hope

"I wait for the Lord, my whole being waits and in His word I put my hope."
Psalm 130:5

We must experience life as Job did—one day at a time and without complete answers to all of life's questions. We live in a fallen world; good behavior is not always rewarded and bad behavior is not always punished. We can have hope in God knowing that the devil does not have free rein over our lives, each test can lead to triumph, and each trial can increase our faith in God.

We have no reason to fear the enemy's tricks because the one who is in you is greater than the one who is in the world. (1 John 4:4) The Holy Spirit and the word of God are in our hearts. While our natural reaction to the troubles we see around us is fear, God's grace can set our sights to see beyond the troubles of the world. We are assured by John that God is stronger than the enemy, and we can trust that truth.

He Is Strong Where We Are Weak

God allows the devil to use both good and bad situations to stretch our faith and encourage us to lean on His word. (James 1:1-3) God loved Paul enough to not allow his pride to cause him to stumble. In 2 Corinthians 12:7, Paul acknowledged the thorn in his flesh as a messenger of Satan, which was sent to keep him from being conceited. His thorn served as a reminder that his help and strength came from God. Paul had a need to stay in constant contact with God, which blessed others as they saw how God was at work in his life. When Paul pleaded with God to remove the thorn, God reassured Paul that His grace is sufficient. (2 Corinthians 12:9) We too can know that when we are humbled by life's trials, we are not alone in the test, and we are more than prepared to stand strong and trust God. God's power shows up in our weakness. We should share our weaknesses, as they can transform a test into triumph and bless others. It's difficult to know when God has been discipling us until we reflect on the situation. Not every misfortune that happens to us comes directly from God. However, He can use guilt, crises, or bad experiences to bring us back to Him if we do not repent of our sins. Difficult times can also come when there are no outstanding sins in our lives. In those seasons, we should be patient and trust God to show us what to do.

In one of Paul's letters to the Corinthian church, he wrote, "I have heard terrible things about some of you. In fact, you are behaving worse than the Gentiles. A man is even sleeping with his own stepmother. You are proud, when you ought to feel bad enough to chase away anyone who acts like that" (1 Corinthians 5:1-2). When we refuse to repent of our sins, our protection from the enemy is compromised, allowing the enemy to attack our lives. In Paul's letter, he told the church that they had a responsibility to maintain the standards of morality found in God's word. God's word tells us not to judge others, but He also tells us not to tolerate flagrant sin that opposes His holiness.

Our Response Is Our Responsibility

Our response to opposition can put us in position to accept or block our blessings. We are told in James to "count it all joy when temptation comes, knowing that the trying of your faith worketh patience" (James 1: 2-3). Our faith can be increased and the lives of others can be changed as witnesses of God's goodness and grace.

The only person we can change can be found in the reflection of a mirror. Our expectations of others can interfere with our growth. We should acknowledge, then release our expectations of others. When we let go of our expectations, we are able to forgive easily. God does not need our help to change any situation, nor anybody. Our hope should be in the ability of God, not in our own strength. We can miss the blessing of a season, by taking for granted the opportunity to increase our faith and dependence on God. The Israelites were in captivity to Egypt, heading through the desert to the Promised Land. Their negative attitudes held them in the desert for forty years when they were on a two-week journey. Constant complaining and griping came from the Israelites along the way. (Exodus 14:11-14) This was a failure of faith. God promotes "gleaners" and holds back those who gripe and refuse to grow. Let go of asking "why;" instead, ask God "what" we are to learn during the season. The secret to peace with God is to discover, accept, and appreciate God's perfect timing.

Have a plan to stay connected with God:

Planning has not always been a strong suit for me. Over time I've learned that it's more beneficial to follow through with a plan than to wing it. Having a plan means that we are more inclined to be intentional with our time. What has worked for me to maintain my hope has been:

1) Start early – Get up early and pray

The concept of starting early fits in many areas of our lives. It means not waiting until snooze has been hit three times, it means not waiting until our schedules allow for prayer time, it means not waiting until we feel like we are drowning before seeking help. Time alone with God is the secret potion to starting the day off right. If we take note of how Jesus spent His time on earth, we will see even He removed Himself from others to hear from the Father. Mark 1:35 illustrates how Jesus used the early morning to get away in solitude to pray. Prayer is a vital link in our communication between ourselves and God. As it was for Jesus, our alone time is necessary to talk to God, and that may mean getting up before the sun.

2) Plan consistently – God has a plan for each of our lives, and if He is wise enough to have a plan, we should follow

suit with our own choices. Having a plan will help us see where we need more help and can lead to us getting help early.

3) Worship with my all – Praise and worship is such a beautiful time to communicate with God. The best moments to surrender happen when the music is drowning out my own thoughts and my all is on the altar.

4) Give yourself grace- There will be times when our plans are interrupted by life. Our intentions are pure, but the day's events may not follow our plan. Resist the urge to get frustrated or discouraged. Some mornings I have my plan set with my day to begin at 5 am, but if I don't rest well the night before my morning routine has to be adjusted. Instead of having my meditation and journal time that morning, I make a sincere effort to have that time before bed.

The Best Decision

We are all born sinners, yet we are saved by God. A fresh outpour of God's love is available to overflow in our lives daily. He wants to live with us every day. As we seek God daily, He pours out His spirit in us. We serve others out of our overflow. Our sin is cleansed in the name of Jesus because of His sacrifice. Only through a relationship with Christ can we have hope in and out of the many seasons of life. Choosing to live for Jesus is an eternal decision. If you have not personally accepted Jesus as your Lord and Savior, I encourage you to make that decision now. Acknowledge that you are a sinner and that through Christ you can be made new. Thank God that He loves you so much that He sent His only Son, a perfect sacrifice, to die on the cross for your sins. The penalty for sin is death, and Jesus paid that penalty for you. Accept His payment for your sins. A simple prayer of acceptance: "Lord Jesus, I need You. Thank You for dying on the cross for my sins. Come into my life. I accept You as my personal Savior and place my trust in You for my salvation. Thank You for forgiving my sins and giving me eternal life. Amen."

> Everyone who drinks this water will be thirsty again, but whoever drinks the water I give him will never thirst, indeed, the water I give him will become in him a spring of water welling up to eternal life.
> (Jn 4:10)

> And the grace of our Lord was exceeding abundant with faith and love which is in Christ Jesus.
> (1 Ti 1:14)

Delight yourself in the Lord, And He will give you the desires of your heart.
(Ps. 37:4)

Seek first the kingdom of God and His righteousness, and all these things will be given to you as well.
(Matt. 6:33)

Because of the Lord's great love, we are not consumed, for His compassions never fail. They are new every morning; great is your faithfulness.
(Lamentations 3:22-23 NIV)

O taste and see that the Lord is good: blessed is the man that trusteth in Him.
(Psalm 34:8)

To Him who is able to keep you from falling and to present you before His glorious presence without fault and with great joy to the only God our Savior be glory, majesty, power, and authority, through Jesus Christ our Lord, before all ages, now and forevermore! Amen.
(Jude 1: 24-25)

Pray in God's Grace

Heavenly Father, we cannot live life without You. We give You our hearts today and ask that You forgive us our sins. Thank You for Your sacrifice on the cross. Today I ask that You fill us with a fresh dose of Your Holy Spirit. God, please bless our first step to see how good You are. Set a deep desire in our hearts to pursue you daily.

www.ingramcontent.com/pod-product-compliance
Lightning Source LLC
Chambersburg PA
CBHW060505080526
44584CB00015B/1560